> **NOT TO BE PUBLISHED**
>
> The information given in this document is not to be communicated, either directly or indirectly, to the Press or to any person not holding an official position in His Majesty's Service.

26/G.S./Pubns./243

> **NOT TO BE TAKEN FORWARD OF FIELD COMPANY HEADQUARTERS**

GERMAN MINES AND TRAPS

FIELD ENGINEERING PAMPHLET No. 2

1940

Printed under the direction of
The Chief of the Imperial General Staff.

THE WAR OFFICE,
February, 1940

The Naval & Military Press Ltd

Published by

The Naval & Military Press Ltd
Unit 5 Riverside, Brambleside
Bellbrook Industrial Estate
Uckfield, East Sussex
TN22 1QQ England

Tel: +44 (0)1825 749494

www.naval-military-press.com
www.nmarchive.com

In reprinting in facsimile from the original, any imperfections are inevitably reproduced and the quality may fall short of modern type and cartographic standards.

CONTENTS

	PAGE
Distribution ..	2

SEC.
1. General—
Description of various groups	3
Points common to all types	4

2. Precautionary measures—
Instructional points	4

3. Booby traps—
General	5
Examples	5
To neutralize traps	5

4. Igniters—
Pull igniter, Z.Z. 35	6
Push igniter, D.Z. 35	7
Combined igniter, Z.D.Z. 29	7
To neutralize an igniter	9

5. The Tellermine—
Description	9
How the mine functions	10
To neutralize the mine	10
To disarm the mine	10

CONTENTS—*continued*

SEC.
6. **Anti-personnel shrapnel mine**—

	PAGE
Description	11
To arm the mine	11
How the mine functions	12
To neutralize the mine	12
To disarm the mine	12

PLATES

NO.
1. Examples of laying Tellermines on roads 13
2. Booby traps behind doors 14
3. Neutralization of igniters 15
4. Pull igniter, Z.Z. 35 16
5. Push igniter, D.Z. 35 17
6.⎫
7.⎭ Combined igniter, Z.D.Z. 29 .. .. 18, 19
8. Tellermine 20
9. Tellermine igniter 21
10.⎫
11.⎭ Anti-personnel shrapnel mine (S-mine, 1935) 22, 23
12. Buried mines, push and pull types 24

DISTRIBUTION

Field squadrons and companies	10	copies
Pioneer battalions	30	,,
Officers cadet training units (Royal Engineers)	100	,,
Royal Engineers training battalions	50	,,

FIELD ENGINEERING PAMPHLET
No. 2—1940

GERMAN MINES AND TRAPS

(compiled from documents issued by French G.Q.G.)

1. GENERAL

1. Up to the present, German mines which have been encountered belong to one of four definite groups.

   i. The elementary booby trap, consisting of a small charge, with an igniter worked by either Push or Pull methods. Some typical examples are described in Sec. **3**.

   ii. Light anti-personnel mines with shrapnel effect, worked by either Push or Pull method. A full description is given in Sec. **6**. Both methods have been used freely, particularly in woods, where it is easier to camouflage the mine. Charges with Pull igniters are usually worked by a simple trip wire, but are often fixed to loose branches and minor hindrances, which the unsuspecting are liable to move. Charges with Push igniters are used generally in combination with an obstacle, being placed in the middle of the obstacle itself and in the approaches to it.

   iii. Light anti-tank mines (Tellermine type). These are generally used on or near roads. Some typical examples are shown in Plate 1. They are usually buried so that the top of the igniter is about two inches below the surface. They can be joined in series by using F.I.D., so that pressure on one mine will explode the whole mine-field. Their browny-chestnut colour harmonises well with the surroundings, so that it is not entirely necessary to bury them. A full description of the mine with its special type of igniter is given in Sec. **5**.

   iv. The heavy anti-tank (box) mines. These are laid in mine-fields usually on roads and tracks. A detailed description of the mine has been given in Field Engineering Pamphlet No. 1. This is a very complicated mine, and should only be neutralized and disarmed by specialists. If it is absolutely necessary to cross mine-fields of this sort, they should either be bridged or destroyed. A charge of two slabs of gun cotton is sufficient to destroy the mine. Care should be taken when approaching these mines as they are usually combined with other booby traps or Tellermines. These mines can also be adjusted to explode under a single man load. No moving parts found should be touched.

2. All German mines and traps have certain points in common. These are :—

  i. All special mines, and slabs or cartridges of explosive have one or more holes drilled and threaded to take the standard igniters described in Sec. 4.

  ii. All igniters can be made safe by means of a nail or piece of wire.

  iii. If plenty of time has been available for their preparation, traps are usually arranged to work by both Push and Pull method.

  iv. Dummy mines, of similar pattern to live ones, are used freely. They should be examined with equal care, as it is difficult to detect that they are dummies, and they may have booby traps attached.

3. In general it is better to neutralize and disarm traps and mines, than to destroy them, as they can then be used against the enemy. When they are found in areas which are occupied for only a short time every effort should be made to add to or reverse existing booby traps, so that the originator may be caught in his own trap.

2. PRECAUTIONARY MEASURES

All troops, likely to come into contact with mines or traps, should be taught certain simple precautionary measures. These are :—

1. When it is suspected that there may be mines or traps about, great care should be taken before any movement is made. Outdoor sites should be examined for trip and tension wires, or disturbed surfaces of the ground. In buildings nothing should be moved until it has been thoroughly examined.

2. When any wire or cord is found it should be followed up, without being touched, to make quite certain that it is not connected to a trap.

3. Any igniters found *must* be neutralized before any wires are cut or unnecessary movements made.

4. All cuts should be made with scissors, rather than a knife, as they do not produce any tension in the cord being cut.

5. Any traps or mines which cannot easily be neutralized should be clearly marked so that they can either be destroyed or dealt with by specially trained men.

6. All screwing or unscrewing of igniters should be done by hand as far as possible. In the case of the Tellermine, it is possible to detonate the mine if the igniter is screwed down more than hand tight.

7. Loose boards, etc., should be regarded with suspicion.

3. BOOBY TRAPS

1. Traps usually consist of tolite charges of two to eight slabs (70 by 50 by 38 mms.; weight $3\frac{1}{4}$ oz.) or cylindrical cartridges (weight $3\frac{1}{2}$ oz.) arranged with Push or Pull igniters.

2. The following are some examples :—

   i. *Doors.* Charges are placed inside houses, over doors, in door frames, or against the wall behind the door when wide open. Doors in such cases are rarely locked, and are sometimes left ajar. Plate 2.

   ii. *Ground floor windows.* Charges are placed on inside sills, and connected to half-open shutters with a wire in tension.

   iii. *Barn doors.* Charges, bigger than the two cases above, are placed on the ground or between battens at the height of a man. These are usually fired by Pull igniters.

   iv. *Miscellaneous.* In cellar entrances, inside doors, cupboards, chests of drawers, farmyard vehicles, loose boards, souvenirs, etc.
   These traps are often marked with distinguishing signs such as a swastika in coloured chalk. The cord or wire which works the igniter is often visible stretched across openings.

3. **To neutralize a trap.**—The first and most delicate operation is to find out where the trap is, and how it is fired. Having discovered the charge, all igniters should be neutralized with split pins or nails. The method

is described at the end of Sec. 4, and is illustrated in Plate 3. Until this has been done great care should be taken to avoid compressing the igniter in any way, or pulling any wires or cords in the vicinity. Once split pins are in position the igniters can safely be unscrewed from the charges. This requires a certain amount of care, as a detonator may be in the igniter tube, and it is liable to fall out.

4. IGNITERS

1. Up to the present three sorts of igniters are known :—

   i. A *Pull* igniter, Z.Z. 35 (Zugzünder 1935).

   ii. A *Push* igniter, D.Z. 35 (Druckzünder 1935).

   iii. A combined igniter, Z.D.Z. 29 (Zugdruckzünder 1929).

Type iii. does not seem to be in use much now. It may have been given up owing to its complexity.

2. **Pull igniter. Z.Z. 35** (Plate 4).—This igniter consists of :—

   i. A brass cylindrical body, which contains all the moving parts and the percussion cap A.

   ii. A percussion assembly consisting of a striker, B, and a spring, C.

   iii. A release mechanism, comprising—

   (a) A sliding cylinder D, which is held in place by a spring E.

   (b) Two short cylindrical pins, F, which slide in a groove cut in the sliding cylinder D, where it contains the striker.

   iv. A safety device consisting of a metal key which passes through a hole in the stem of the sliding cylinder and two holes G in the body of the igniter.

   When in repose (position shown in Plate 4) the pins F engage in a groove in the striker, and are held in place there by a bulge I on the main body.

   When the end H is pulled the internal cylinder slides in the main body. After it has moved a certain amount the pins F are freed from the bulge on the body. The upper side of the groove, in which the pins F move, is cut on a bevel. This, under pressure of the striker spring, causes the pins to fly outwards, and so release the striker.

3. **Push igniter. D.Z. 35** (Plate 5).—The igniter consists of :—
   i. A cylindrical body of varnished aluminum, which contains all the moving parts, and the percussion cap A.
   ii. A percussion assembly consisting of a striker B, and a spring C.
   iii. A release mechanism consisting of—
      (a) A sliding cylinder D held in place by a spring E, which bears on a bulge D^1.
      (b) Two ball bearings F, which are free to move in a groove in the body D.
   iv. A safety device consisting of a metal key which passes through a hole in the body D.

   When in repose (position shown in Plate 5) the ball bearings engage in a cut in the stem of the striker, which has its upper side rebated, and are held in position by a bulge on the body D.

   When any pressure is brought to bear on the head H, the sliding cylinder is depressed. This frees the ball bearings, which fly outwards under the pressure of the striker spring, and so release the striker.

4. **Combined igniter. Z.D.Z. 29** (Plates 6 and 7).
   i. The igniter consists of :—
      (a) A body A, having a slit S for the safety key J (beneath the slit is engraved the word SICH), and two holes for the safety pin (Pull) K (beneath these is the word ZUG).
      (b) The detonator tube H with its percussion cap. This is screwed into the main body, and held in place by the pin I.
         A striker guide B fixed with two screws to the body A. This guide has—
         (i.) An aperture for the safety key J.
         (ii.) A hole for the safety pin K.
         (iii.) Two external stops R and R^1.
         (iv.) Two internal gudgeons L and L^1.
      (c) A striker C, with a cylindrical seating D^1 for the striker spring D. (This spring is always compressed by the adjustable button F). A circular groove M, a small cut O, and a large cut P.

(d) An adjustable button F, comprising—

    (i.) On its top, the word DRUCK, a datum cut N, and a slot which can be turned by a screwdriver or a coin.

    On its underside, a seating F^1 for the striker spring, a pin O^1 which fits into the slit Y, and a stop Q which butts against the stops R and R^1 in the extreme positions of the adjustable button.

(e) A bush E for holding the button F, with three slits for the safety key J, the gudgeon A^1 and the safety pin K. On the top of the bush are three marks: ZUG, 125 Kgs and 45 Kgs: below each of which there is a hole to receive the stop Q.

(f) A bush G for fixing the assembly E and F, screwed to the body A.

Use as a PUSH igniter.—

(a) Set the datum cut N on the adjustable button against the marks 125 Kgs or 45 Kgs. The Pull safety pin should be in the large cut P.

(b) Remove the safety key J.
The device is then armed.

When the button (set at 45 Kgs) is depressed, the striker body cuts the gudgeon L (which is of soft metal), and the striker spring then forces the striker down on to the percussion cap.

When set at 125 Kgs, both gudgeons L and L^1 have to be cut, before the spring can function.

iii. Use as a PULL igniter.—

(a) Set the datum cut N against the word ZUG. In this position gudgeon L is in the slot P, and L^1 is in slot O; the safety pin K alone holds the striker by engagement in the groove M.

(b) Remove the safety key J.
The device is then armed. If the safety pin K is withdrawn the striker will function.

NOTE.—When the device is set at ZUG, if the safety pin K is withdrawn leaving the safety key J in place, the striker will not move. If, however, an attempt is made to remove the safety key J as well it will only move a short distance, as the point of the striker will engage in a slot in the key. It is then impossible to withdraw the key, or to make the device function.

To neutralize any igniter, it is only necessary to insert a split pin, nail or similar article through the safety pin holes.

5. THE TELLERMINE
Plates 8 and 9.

1. **Description.**

This mine weighs 19 lb. and contains about 11 lb. of tolite. It is circular, diameter about 1 foot, with convex top and flat bottom, its height being about 4 inches. A handle is provided on one side for easy carriage.

It consists of :—

i. A cylindrical box A filled with tolite. This has a hole B in the top designed to take :—

   (a) The detonator C. The upper part is painted red.

   (b) A leather washer and some metal washers.

   (c) A spring E on which the lid of the mine rests.

   It also has two other holes, F and G, which are threaded to take the standard igniter, should it be desired to add extra booby traps. They will also take F.I.D., which is the method used to join up a series of mines.

ii. A cover H in pressed metal, with a circular rubber collar round its edge to make a good joint with the main body. The cover has a central hole into which the firing device is screwed.

iii. A metallic belt K which fixes the lid to the body.

iv. An ignition device which comprises—

   (a) The body A, threaded to screw into the cover, with a rubber washer. Its cap B^1 just bears on the top of the detonator.

   (b) A percussion device, consisting of a sliding body C^1 and a striker D^1 with its spring. The sliding body and the striker are held together by a shearing pin G^1.

v. There are two safety devices in this igniter provided by means of—

    (a) A safety pin F^1 inserted through the hole E.

    (b) A bulge I^1 on the bottom of the striker, which prevents its movement. The position of this bulge is controlled by the screw head H^1. This has a red spot on it which can be turned to SICHER (safe) or SCHARF (danger), as required. On some patterns the words SICHER and, SCHARF are replaced by white and red spots respectively.

2. How the mine functions.

When any load presses on the cover of the mine the spring E is depressed. The igniter presses on the washers in the hole B. This tends to press the sliding body C^1 of the igniter upwards. If the pressure is sufficient the pin G^1 is sheared. This frees the striker, which strikes the cap, which in turn causes the detonator to function.

3. To neutralize the mine.

    i. Examine the area round the mine for additional traps and, if found, neutralize them.

    ii. Put a split pin into the hole E.

    iii. Examine sides and bottom of mine, without moving it, to see if any additional igniters are in holes F and G. When these have been neutralized, the mine is reasonably safe.

4. To disarm the mine.

    i. Unscrew any additional igniters, and extract the detonators from the holes.

    ii. Unscrew the main igniter.

DO NOT—

1. Try to turn the screw H^1 to safe until the igniter has been removed from the mine.

2. Try to remove the main central detonator until well clear of the mine field. This is a specialist's job, as these detonators are particularly sensitive.

6. ANTI-PERSONNEL SHRAPNEL MINE
Plates 10, 11 and 12.

1. Description.

This mine is a cylinder of diameter 10 cm. and height 14·5 cm. It weighs about 9 lb. and contains about 1 lb. of tolite and 350 steel bullets. Inside the outer cover A, there is a pressed steel cylinder B, 2mm. thick. This slides easily in the outer envelope. It rests on a metal disc C, which is fixed to the outer cover by three screws D.

The charge T is in a movable cylinder E, which contains one central tube F and three other parallel tubes H, screwed to the disc C. At the bottom of the central tube is a small device G, which contains a train of powder. This leads to the recess R, which contains about 2 grammes of powder.

The plate K, which is the envelope cover, has the following holes :—

    i. Central hole through which the tube F passes.

    ii. Hole L, which has a screw plug of 15 mm. diameter, for filling.

    iii. Three holes M, which have screw plugs 10 mm. diameter.

The plate is held in place by a lock nut N. Between the plate and the shrapnel bullets is some string packing.

In addition at the top end of the central tube the following can be screwed.

        (*a*) A special piece in the form of a junction with three tubes sticking out, of which two will hold *Pull* igniters (Plate 12)

    or (*b*) a *Pull* igniter.

        (*c*) a *Push* igniter.

2. To arm the mine.

    i. Close down cover plate K.

    ii. Unscrew three plugs M.

    iii. Slide a detonator into each tube H, with its opening pointing downwards.

    iv. Screw in three plugs M.

    v. Fix igniter.

How the mine functions.

When the igniter fires, the flame produced goes down the central tube and lights the powder train G. This explodes the small powder charge R, which throws the inner cylinder B into the air. At the same time it fires the detonators in the tubes H, which explode the charge. The delay in detonation of the main charge permits the casing to rise 2 to 3 feet into the air before exploding. The shrapnel bullets are effective up to a range of about 150 yards to 200 yards.

Two methods of using the mine are shown in Plate 12.

It should be noted that when the mine is to be fired under pressure, three steel antennæ are fixed to the igniter. These are 3 cm. long, and their upper ends should be level with the surface of the ground.

4. To neutralize the mine.

   i. *Pull igniters, with trip wires showing—*

   (a) Release the wires from the head of the igniters, which are usually above ground. Be careful not to pull the wires.

   (b) Put split pins or nails through the safety pin holes of the igniters.

   ii. *Push igniters—*

   (a) Remove, with care, the steel antennæ.

   (b) Put split pin or nail through the safety pin hole.

5. To disarm the mine.

   i. Unscrew the igniters.

   ii. Unscrew the three plugs M.

   iii. Extract the detonators by turning the mine over gently, and tapping it on the bottom.

NOTE.—**These mines should never be stacked, unless they have been disarmed.**

MINE LAYING

PLATE 1

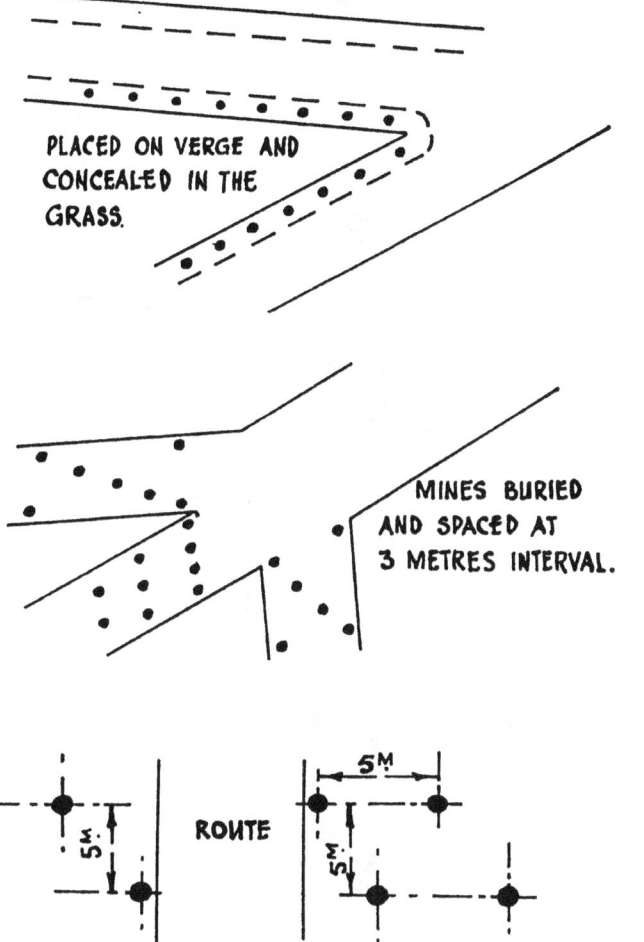

PLATE 2

BOOBY TRAPS
(Placed behind doors.)

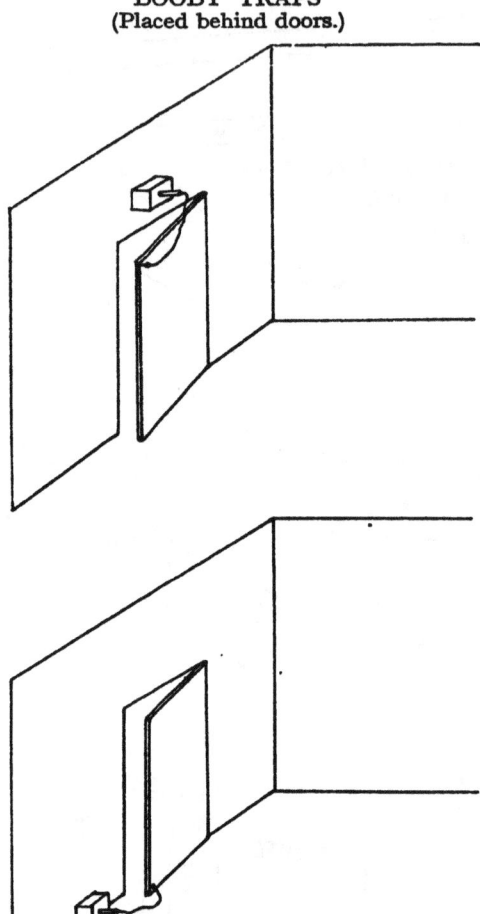

NEUTRALIZATION OF IGNITERS

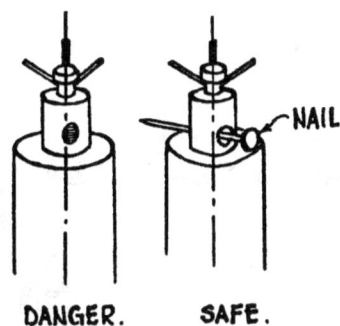

FIG. 1.—Push igniters.

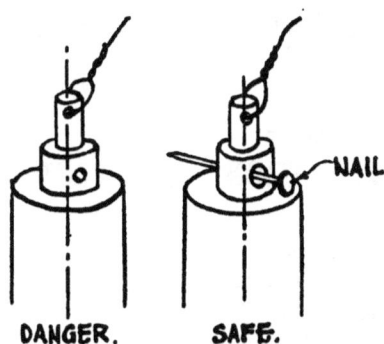

FIG. 2.—Pull igniters.

PLATE 4

PULL IGNITER, Z.Z. 35

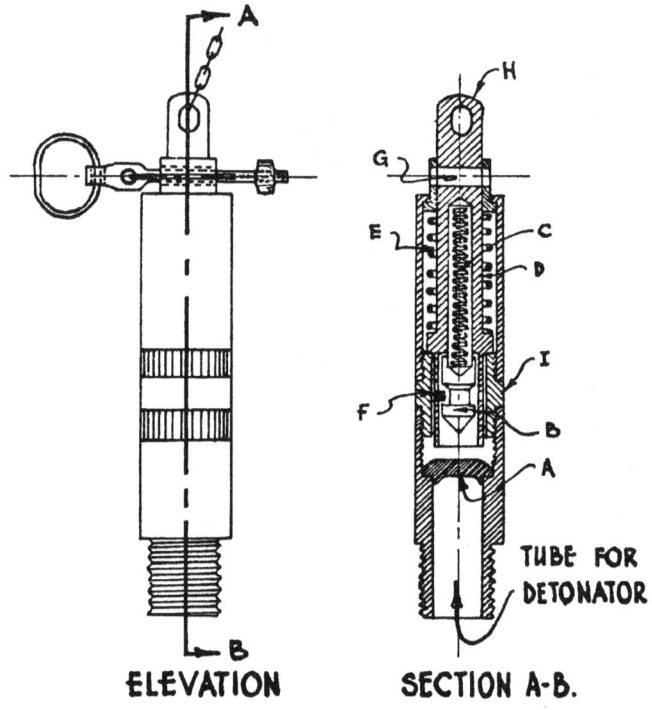

ELEVATION

SECTION A-B.

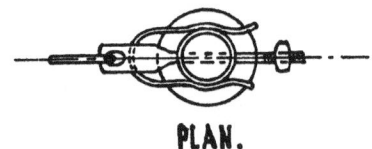

PLAN.

PUSH IGNITER, D.Z. 35

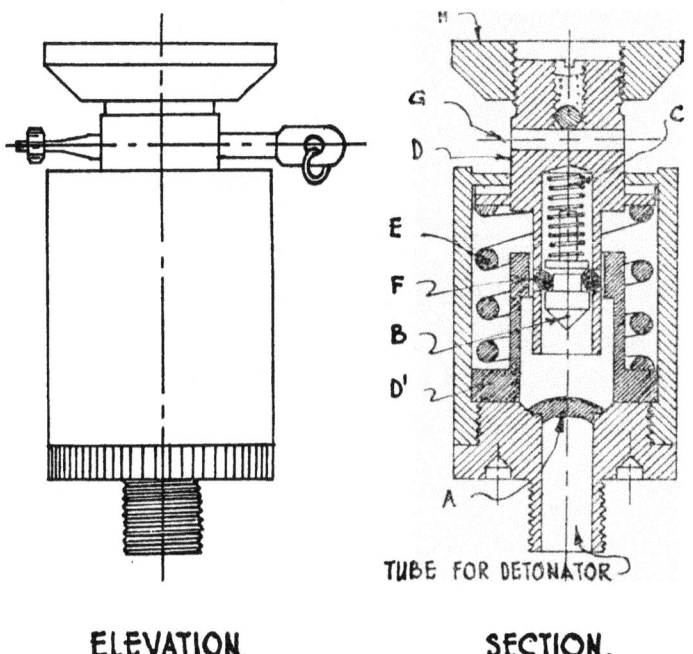

ELEVATION.   SECTION.

PLATE 6

COMBINED IGNITER, Z.D.Z. 29

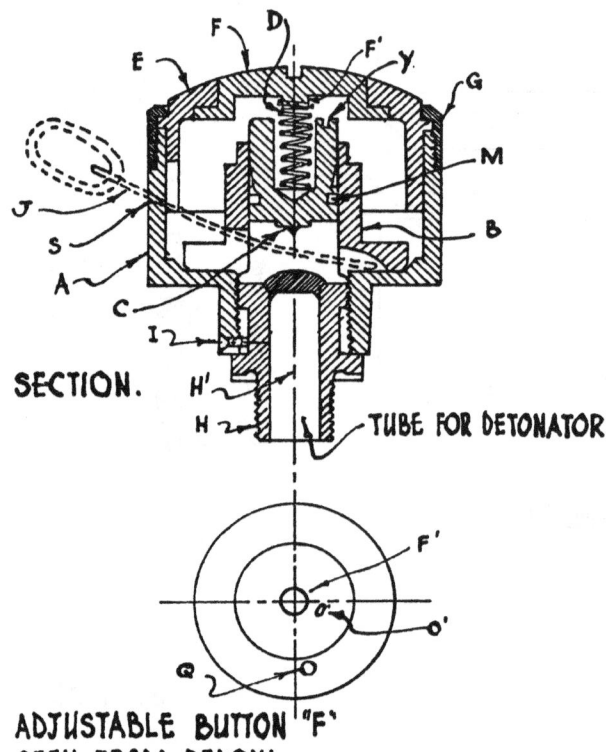

SECTION.

TUBE FOR DETONATOR

ADJUSTABLE BUTTON "F" SEEN FROM BELOW.

COMBINED IGNITER, Z.D.Z. 29 — PLATE 7

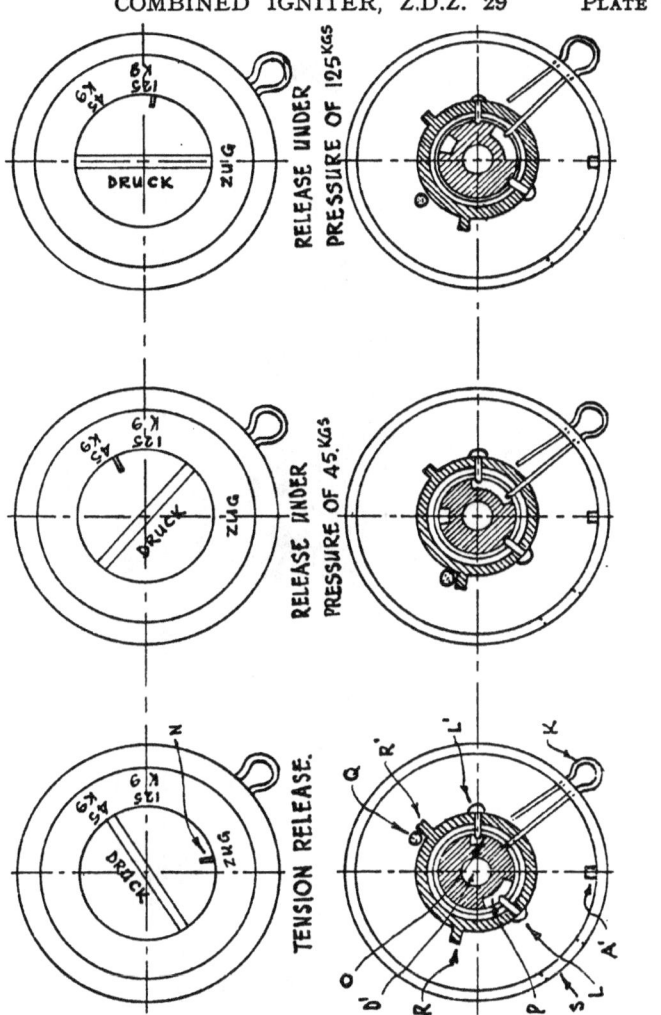

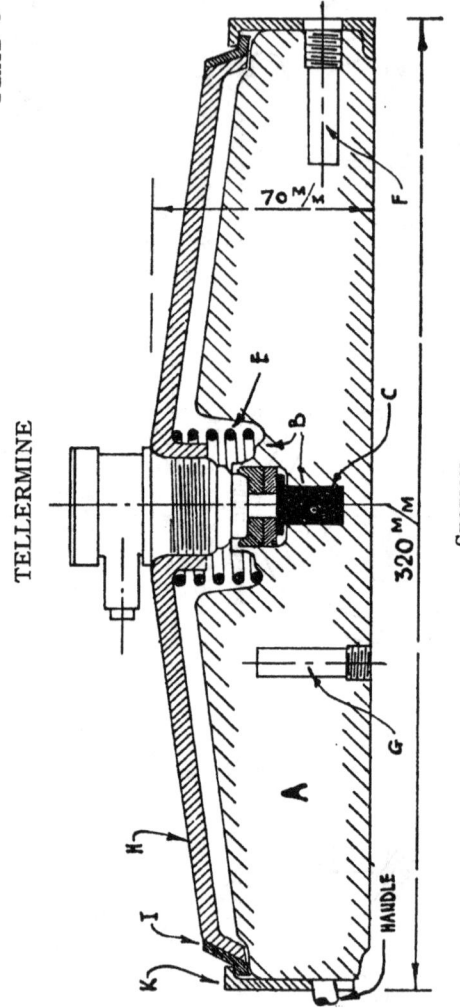

IGNITER, TELLERMINE

PLATE 9

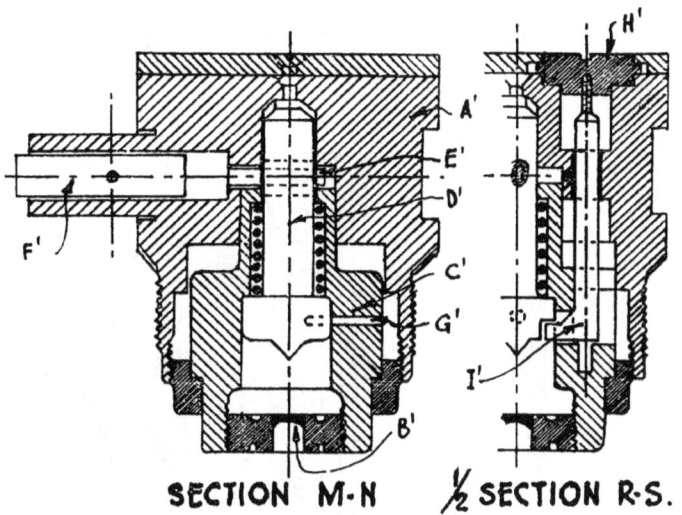

SECTION M-N   ½ SECTION R-S.

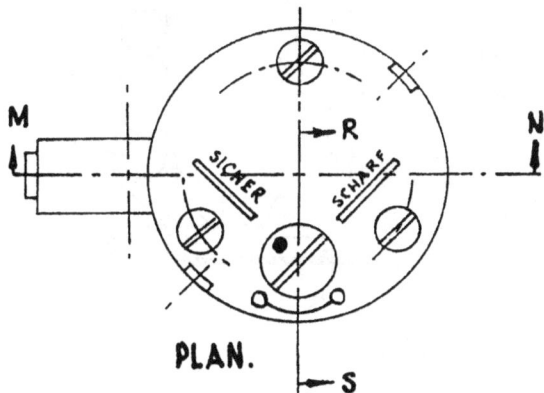

PLAN.

PLATE 10

ANTI-PERSONNEL SHRAPNEL MINE
(S-Mine, 1935.)

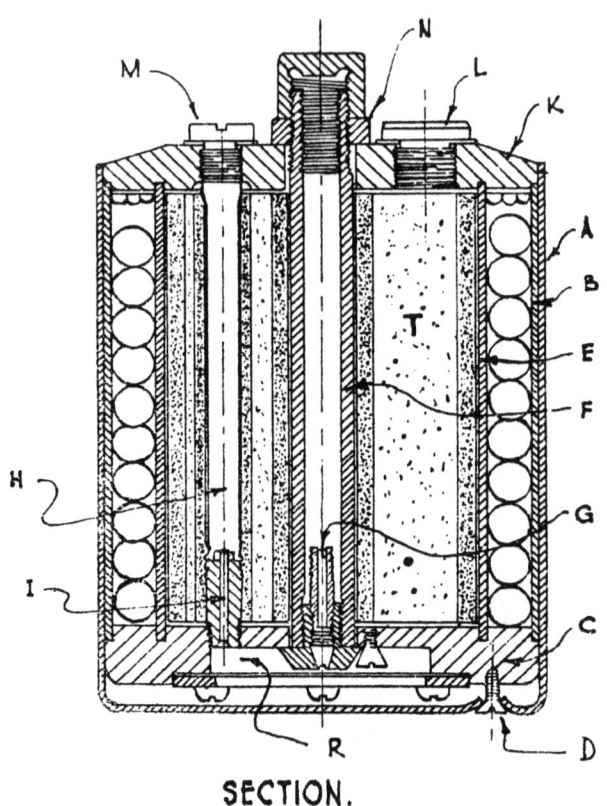

SECTION.

ANTI-PERSONNEL SHRAPNEL MINE PLATE 11
(S-Mine, 1935.)

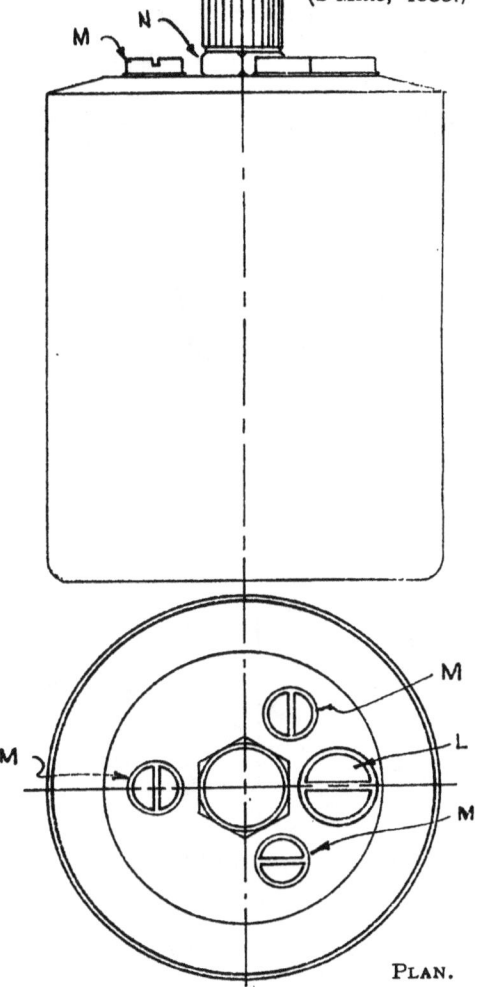

PLAN.

PLATE 12

BURIED MINES

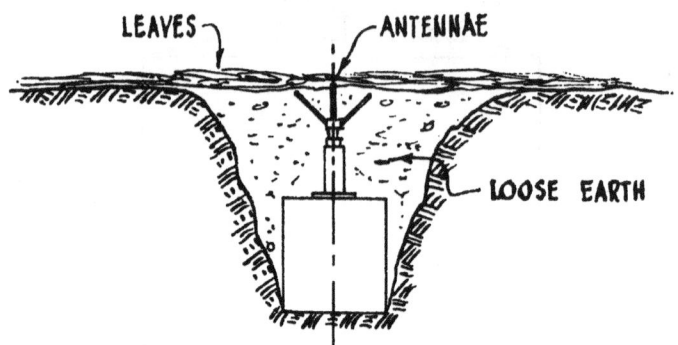

Fig. 1.—Push mine.

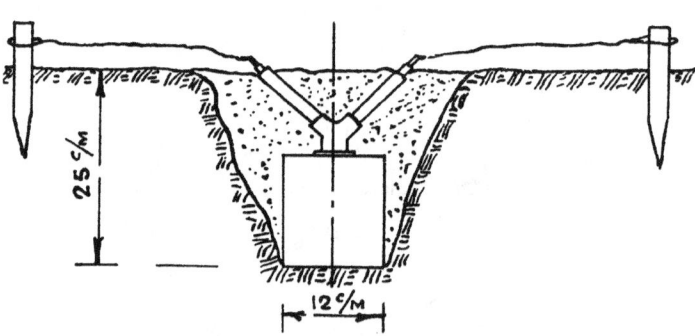

Fig. 2.—Pull mine.

Printed under the Authority of HIS MAJESTY'S STATIONERY OFFICE
į (2/40). Wt. 17527—8202. 2,000. 6/40. (1768). W. C. & S. Ltd. **Gp. 394.**

www.ingramcontent.com/pod-product-compliance
Lightning Source LLC
Chambersburg PA
CBHW070456050426
42450CB00012B/3299